D0913460

THE

COMMUNITY

OF

SELF

(Revised)

BY NA'IM AKBAR, PH.D.

MIND

PRODUCTIONS

MIND PRODUCTIONS & ASSOCIATES, INC.
P. O. BOX 11221
TALLAHASSEE, FL 32302

Copyright 1985 by Na'im Akbar

Sixteenth printing: August 2008

Cover design: Abdul Majied

Published by *Mind Productions & Associates, Inc.*
Tallahassee, FL 32304

Library of Congress catalog No: 95-079376
ISBN: 0~935257~00~4

Printed in the United States of America

Acknowledgements

There are many people who deserve credit for this revision of *The Community of Self*. The most significant contribution has come from Abdul Hasib Matin of New York City. Abdul is a poet and writer in his own right and because of his outstanding skills as a journalist, his voluntary editing of the entire manuscript makes this book much better than its predecessor. He spent hours laboring over the manuscript of this book, coming to Florida to discuss it with me, expending considerable self-initiated effort to make the book successful. His suggestions have been invaluable and he is actually responsible for insuring that this project would get done. My sincerest thanks to Abdul Hasib Matin for his efforts in making this happen.

We also extend our thanks to Imam Waarith Deen Mohammed whose *Qur'anically* inspired ideas offered the initial inspiration and much valuable insight which assisted me in developing the ideas which are discussed in this book. We know, however, that no concepts of Truth have an individual source, but are reflections of the basics that have come from the Creator. So, we are grateful to Allah (God) for this opportunity and for these ideas.

To my office staff who works patiently and with great loyalty, I must extend my thanks. Especially to Rosalyn Nix who did all of the typing and to my executive secretary, Gloria Mu'min, who hangs with me through the "thick and thin," I appreciate your hard work. Byron, Dwayne, and Spencer keep things moving in the office of *Mind Productions*.

None of my efforts occur without the support and sacrifices of my family. To my children Shaakira, Mutaqee and Tareeq; my father Luther B. Weems; and the spiritual presence of my ancestors, especially my mother, Bessie G. King, and my aunt, Eunice Carter, I extend my sincerest thanks for your love and support.

Table of Contents

Introduction

This little book was initially conceived and written in early 1976. It was a product of my efforts in developing a concept for my Office of Human Development for the (then) Nation of Islam. The Office of Human Development no longer exists, neither does that version of the Nation of Islam. My desire to develop a meaningful and useful concept of human development that will be liberating for human beings persists. Three other small books followed this one in its original form, each attempting to tackle some aspect of the very complicated problems confronted by human beings in this time and in this place. Because of my primary commitment to the too-often ignored African-American tribe of which I am a proud member, my efforts have most often been directed to that population.

The human dilemma does not come in colors, races or nationalities, but the dilemma takes on particular qualities as a result of those characteristics. Particularly here in North America, one cannot discuss the human condition without identifying the ethnic or racial qualities of the group under consideration. It has become increasingly clear, however, that there are universal principles of human development which have relevance to all human beings in all times and in all places, but they must be discussed in the context of the environmental realities which define or distort the concept of peoplehood.

Oddly enough, *The Community of Self* was the smallest of the books that I have done and in many ways is the most general of the group. Despite this, however, it has been the most popular. Many, many people in all walks of life have commented that this small booklet did more to help them see themselves in a clear light than anything they had ever read. My desire was for the book to be of service and it seemed to have accomplished that goal.

After five printings, the book was taken out of print around 1979 because of a growing concern that the language of the book was clumsy and confusing. It was initially written as a testimonial to the ideas of Imam W. Deen Muhammad. In my zeal to be appropriately respectful of his inspiration, the book's language did not flow and the context of the ideas was rather encumbered by a proselytizing tone.

Therefore, many people who did not understand the (then) Nation of Islam and its subsequent changes could not relate to the book. For a number of years I have been encouraged to rewrite the book, and at last, I have had an opportunity to do so, with some expansion and clarification, while remaining true to the better ideas in the earlier form.

A play was written by my very dear friend, Adib Shakir, back in the latter part of 1976. The play was an excellent rendering of the major ideas from *The Community of Self* and it served as an outstanding teaching aid for both children and adults about their make-up as people. At last, psychology was coming alive for me. After years of study, I had remained frustrated and dissatisfied that psychology was something that seemed to belong to scholars and those with many years of training in the language and techniques of the field. There was not much access to the information as an instrument to cultivate self-knowledge because of the complexity of the concepts and the difficulty of the language. Only the experts had a grasp (and not a very good one) on what the human make-up was about and what was entailed in developing one's self.

Adib Shakir's play entitled *The Community of Self* permitted people of all ages to see their inner make-up dramatically and musically played out before their very eyes. It was psychodrama for the masses of people. People were able to be entertained, instructed and assisted in correcting distortions in their lives simultaneously. The book, because of its intentionally simple language and small size, had already captured the interest of large numbers of people who had never seen a psychology book and now the play made it even more meaningful. Art, science, psychology and religion had all come together and this was the essence of human development.

This revision represents some maturation in my thinking as well as expansion of the concepts which were developed almost ten years ago. The effort has been to remain consistent with the earlier concept to be clear, simply and readable to as wide an audience as possible. *The Community of Self* was never intended to be a scholarly production addressed to only experts in the field of psychology. It was intended to be a tool whereby human beings can help themselves, understand themselves, and grow themselves. It has grown out of a lingering conviction that knowledge of self is the key to human power and effectiveness. It represents only one in a series of such efforts to help bring clarity to this concept to the very best of my ability.

Developing a liberating concept of human development represents one of the real challenges of this terminating 20th century. Technology in the modern world has far surpassed its psychology. Our speed and efficiency in moving, communicating and processing information has gone considerably beyond our understanding of ourselves, our human condition and our responsibility. Human relationships have seriously deteriorated from a higher level at periods of less technological advancement. There is more personal unhappiness, dissatisfaction and frustration than existed when material resources were much less developed. The most advanced nations, technologically, seem to be the most undeveloped ones humanly. There seems to be diminishing concern for the weaker person and an insensitivity to the aspirations of the needy. Basic moral life is in jeopardy in the wake of expanding individualism and relative ethics which encourage people to do their thing with little concern for the collective good or even the natural laws.

One solution that recommends itself in the wake of these human difficulties is the need for a revolutionary concept of human development. People no longer know their nature as human beings and have even less respect for their responsibility as thinking beings. Self-knowledge is at an all-time low and with it is human dignity. Right wing evangelism won't solve the problem though there is a need for a revival in the moral values of Western people. People will not grow when they are intimidated into moral control because of a fear of hell, fire and damnation. Human dignity grows and remains strong when people are encouraged to understand their own human processes, development and the interaction of those processes with the natural flow of the cosmos. People with such understanding respect good conduct and follow it as a definition of survival and progress. Fear as an instrument of moral conduct simply drives people away from the feared situation and encourages them to defy the moral standards of the threat as soon as they feel free.

The Community of Self talks about yourself, myself, ourselves. The context is the African-American experience, not to reduce the generalization of the concepts to one group of people, but because this is my cultural context. The African-American experience stands as one of the strongest examples of high human principles being able to endure despite environments of extreme opposition, and there is instruction in what we can offer the world without being human. Because of the seriousness of the assault on the African-American, our situation is also precarious. We need the attention of our thinkers for ourselves.

We need to restore our communities and to understand and develop our communities of self. We need assistance in correcting some serious problems in our psychology, our education, our economics, our families and our religious thinking. *The Community of Self* addresses all of these areas. It is intended to provoke thought and action. It is intended to stimulate an improved understanding of who we are, what we are and our potential to be something as valuable to the world as we have been before and are destined to be again.

THE COMMUNITY OF SELF

The Self is a kind of community. It has within it the specialists which one finds within any community. These specialists perform certain important functions for the benefit of the whole community. The road to inner peace is the same road to outer peace. Such peace is acquired by harmonious cooperation of these members under a leadership for the common good.

MOTORS OF THE SELF

Among the earliest citizens in the self community are the drives or instincts. They are called drives because they are movers of the self. They are sometimes called instincts because people are born with these drives. Drives are not taught, though the object or goal of the drives is learned by people.

All of these drives can be included under two major types or classes. One type of drive is movement towards what gives pleasure or satisfaction. The other drive is the reverse in that it moves one away from what causes pain or dissatisfaction. These drives are the mental speakers for the physical body and its needs. Those things necessary for physical survival require mental representation.

Food, for example, is necessary for human physical survival. Since food brings pleasure or satisfaction to a hungry person, we are naturally attracted to food. Hunger causes pain or dissatisfaction, so the person is driven away from conditions that cause hunger, i.e., an empty stomach.

Anything that causes damage to the physical borders of the self is experienced as painful. Cuts, burns, collisions, etc., are all potentially damaging to the physical parts of the self. When such threats to the physical self are present, the entire community becomes immediately motivated for *fight* or *flight*. The entire physical self and mental self is alerted by such threats: the memory, reason, senses and ego all focus their specialized capacities on the threat.

Memory of previous dangers and previously dangerous situations and people can set off the same threat avoidance alarm as occurs when the real danger is present. This causes anxiety or fear.

Very often we are nervous or anxious simply because we are in the presence of a person or situation which was threatening at some other time.

Anything present when we experience pleasure can become pleasurable. We then learn to seek anything that may have brought pleasure in the past. Money is not directly pleasurable, but because it provides for many physical pleasures, most people are driven to acquire money.

The drives are very necessary, especially for the physical survival of the person. They attract us to what sustains us or perpetuates us physically. They move us away from the things that may physically damage us.

If the drives are permitted to rule the self, the person becomes only a physical pleasure-seeker. They are concerned only with what brings physical pleasure: food, sex, physical relaxation. If the drives are given free rein, they will drive the entire community to seek only pleasure. Fear can come to rule and the person is constantly nervous or anxious in their persistent drive to avoid pain.

Rulership by the drives can be very limiting because the person is bound by physical pleasures and pains. If wo/man is defined as *mind*, the person ruled by demands of the body is not a man or a woman.

SENSES IN THE SELF COMMUNITY

Almost at the time of birth, the person begins to establish contact with the outer world by way of the body's windows known as the senses. The senses are another very important part of the community of self. Sight, hearing, smell, taste and touch are the channels through which the self receives messages from the outer world. Without these windows into the world, the community of self would be locked behind a wall of darkness, silence and complete isolation from the beautiful and informative physical world which surrounds us.

The senses are to the community of self what communication is to communities of people. It is the basis of contact. Without such contact, there could be no exchange; there would be no growth within the community.

Senses add to the drives the direction for proper physical maintenance. They orient towards those objects which satisfy the drives. They also provide windows into the relationship between the inner life of the self community and the outer world.

It is through these senses that humans can gain some satisfaction by the sensory relationship between inner needs and outer objects. These inner needs may emanate from the body or other parts of the mind's community.

The processes of the physical world are also a source of instruction for the development of the inner life. Observation of these processes is an essential part of learning how they work and making them a part of our own growth.

There is no doubt that the senses are a critical part of the *community of self.* But if the community relies on the senses as the ruler of self, then the self will suffer. The senses give only incomplete information about things. Often, that which appeals to the senses might endanger the self community. The senses often deceive, in that they only provide surface information about the environment. The senses are ineffective in making judgments of the world and are equipped to guide only by impression. Even those impressions are often shaped by other parts of the mind's community. We must conclude that the senses are an important part of the community, but they make a poor ruler over the self.

EMOTIONAL EGO

Another prominent citizen in the circle of the self community is the ego. The ego is the part of the self that speaks up for the rights of the individual. The ego's specialized function is to make sure that the individual needs of the person's self are not being violated. It approaches the environment looking for support of the individual person. The ego also remains sharply tuned for dangers to the self community.

The tool used by the ego is emotion. The strong feelings which well up from the inside of a person usually is the voice of the ego. It responds to support and attention by feelings of pride and love. It responds to threat and neglect by sadness or hatred.

The ego has the capacity to involve and affect the entire community by its emotional alarms. Everything one sees or hears is more beautiful when the ego is feeling love. Everything seems gray and cloudy when it is sad. Many pleasant memories are recalled when ego is happy. Many maddening memories rush to consciousness when ego is disturbed. When gripped by emotions, reasoning fails to function adequately.

Ego is vital for the life of the community. When ego is not adequately developed, the entire community of self fails to support itself. One serious consequence of the slavery and societal oppression of African-Americans was the retardation of the ego. When ego is retarded, people don't like themselves. When ego is retarded, people destroy themselves directly and indirectly without caring. When ego is retarded, it fails to motivate the memory to remember and the senses, reasoning, and other members of the community fall down on their job.

The ego can also be a tyrannical ruler over the community. If it seizes control of the community, the entire self is forced to work for the individual needs only. The person sees and hears only what it wants to sense. People can then remember only what they want to remember. They become unable to reason objectively, instead, things are analyzed only as they affect the almighty *I*.

Because the ego's only weapon is emotions, people ruled by ego become air-like people. These people are easily excited. They fall in and out of love easily. They become angry easily. They are easily offended and they will cooperate with other "communities" (people) only if it benefits themselves.

The ego is an actor. Its experience is primarily conscious, so it fails to involve itself with things which it cannot see. Ego changes its face and allegiance as selfish needs dictate. It is always committed to the best outcome for the person, but it is a terrible ally for either other communities or wiser and more socially conscious parts of its own community. So, again, we have found a necessary citizen of the community, but it is clearly not an appropriate ruler over the self.

MEMORY

Another important member of the community of self is the memory. It is like the library or the archives of a mighty city. It stores the many records of experience which have gone into the building of the person. From these records of the memory, the person is guided by the light of previous lessons and rises above previous mistakes. The memory is a loyal community worker so long as it does not seek to rule.

If the memory loses sight of its position as a resource and seeks to dominate the community of self, the self ceases to grow and lives in the chambers of the past. Memory sometimes loses sight of its proper position as a foundation for the present and tries to exert its influence over the future. When this happens, the self finds itself imprisoned by old memories and past experiences. Such imprisonment destroys life because the self keeps looking at the present as if it were the past. The past becomes the ruler and the self repeats the old patterns of living over and over.

We must constantly strive to identify the proper ruler for our *community of self.* We can recognize the proper ruler of the community because it is the one whose interest is not for personal advancement, but for the total advancement of the community.

We can easily see, then, that memory is an important part of the community. In fact, without memory, there would be little continuity in the community. But we can also see that if memory rules the community, the community lives in the past.

ORGANIZATION IN THE SELF

Another important member of selfhood is reason. Reason works along with other members in the self community. Reason has a most important role in the community as do the drives, senses, ego, and the memory. Reason brings order and organization to the information brought in by the senses. With reason, we know that everything which is green is not grass. With reason, we know that our senses give us incomplete information about the world. With reason, we also use time to help us make effective judgments. We are able to distinguish between yesterday's experience and today's reality. We are equipped with reason to classify experiences in terms of time, space, quality, and other dimensions. Reason gives meaning or interpretation to experiences. Because of its order, reason helps make the environment predictable and more manageable.

The reasoning activity in the community of self works throughout the community keeping order and organization. If the reasoning, however, tries to rule the community, the self becomes like a machine. The self would be unable to enjoy the good things of the senses because the reason would always try to put life and the world in some category or class. There would be no humor because funny things usually are unexpected. There would be no surprises because complete order would make everything predictable. There would be no real enjoyment because reason would always be classifying and qualifying. Reason can be cold and unfeeling. It judges the world on the basis of category or characteristic only. It fails to consider sensitive inner needs. It fails to consider factors which are not always observable. Reason is also insensitive to moral imperatives. It judges only on the basis of the facts.

Therefore, reason is an important citizen in the community of self. There can be no self without some order. But, if unfeeling order seeks to rule the self, it will destroy peace and happiness within the self.

THE SELF-ACCUSING SPIRIT

The *community of self* becomes a community of justice as the conscience begins to develop. The conscience is a very important member of the community in that it polices all components of the self. The conscience introduces a value of good or bad, right or wrong, to the senses' observation of the environment around them. It even exercises control over the drives for pleasure and avoidance of pain by the same value dimension. Its power is so great that pleasure can be denied for extended periods because the denial is valued as good. Considerable pain can be endured in the name of right.

The ego which concerns itself only with the needs of *I*, surrenders under the power of a developed conscience which restrains the I for the good of the We. Even the organizational sense called reason, which usually dominates by its rigid consistency, bows under the tempering influence of that sense of right and wrong.

The conscience or **self-accusing spirit**, as it is called in the *Holy Qur'an* (the holy book of the Muslims), is the moral sense in the person. It helps us to maintain justice within ourselves while guiding us to seek justice with other selves. It moves beyond the simple mental function of determining what is and what is not. It urges us to choose directions based on what is good for the wider community of minds in which the mind (wo/man) finds itself. It is observant of self, but urges sacrifice of ego for the wider self. It urges the self towards the development and enhancement of the highest possibilities for itself.

Without the conscience, the community of self would have no upward direction. The community would operate only on the basis of what is sensed with its senses or desired with its drives; it would strive to please its ego or follow its memorized reason or organization. The community would have no basis for improving itself because there would be nothing to guard itself against self-indulgence.

An unchecked conscience, however, can be as disruptive to the self community as the other parts previously discussed. Rather than a gentle urging to improvement, the over-developed conscience can demand nothing short of perfection. Its self-sacrificing tendency can become greedy for punishment. This leads to a constant state of dissatisfaction within the self community. This guiding sense of wrong can become a constant condemnation of every thought, every weakness, every drive rising from the lower self. Such strong and punitive demands can weaken the whole community into a community of self-hatred. Much of the chronic sadness or depression and even suicides sometimes come from a too demanding conscience. The moral sense is not an end itself, but it is the guide to the higher sense. The self-accusing spirit is a highly placed messenger of the ruler, but it hasn't the restraint to rule the community.

THE RULER OVER SELF

All creatures on the earth operate under the force of instinct or natural law. The unique feature which distinguishes humans from all other parts of the creation is Will. The human Will frees us from the limitations of our drives unlike any other animal. Our power to create lies in our Will and its ability to aspire beyond what is immediately available. The *will power* has the unique ability to pull the mind and flesh in the direction of Truth.

Unlike the other parts of the self community, which are all geared to achieve their separate goals, the Will is set to organize and harmonize all components of the self. The Will draws upon the functions of all parts of the community and unites those separate forces for the good of the whole self community.

The Will is also our fallibility or shortcoming because it is our limited free will which permits us to fall victim to other parts of the self. When other parts of the self are permitted to grow too strong, they seize control of the Will and use it for their separate functions. By education and purification of the Will, which gives freedom from negative influences from other parts of the self, humans are capable of great heights of growth.

So the Will, which is the Divine representative within the person when working with the higher parts of conscience and guided by proper direction, is the intended "Khalifah," or ruler over the self community. When the Will achieves rulership over the self, the self grows to be the proper ruler over the earth.

Once the self has achieved proper rulership within itself, it has come into proper and harmonious organization as well. The establishment of such inner organization is the foundation for establishing an outer community of harmony and organization for the entire world.

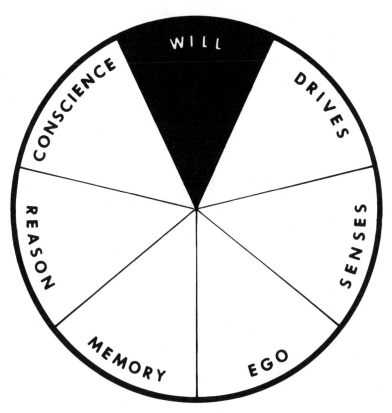

Illustration of the components of the Self Community ruled over by the Will

DEVELOPING

RESPONSIBILITY FOR SELF

One of the main problems that we face as human beings in modern America is a declining sense of responsibility for our own lives. Living in a society where the influences are so powerful, it is very difficult to hear the voice of our own inner power.

The volume of external influences, such as television, popular music and other cultural inputs, overwhelm us. Bombarded by fashions, foods and fads, our appetites remain highly aroused. With images of self-indulgence, such as adultery, deception, greed and corruption, it becomes difficult to imagine life in any other form. With songs of seduction and easy drug availability, we begin to conclude that these impulses cannot be controlled, but are the inevitable result of living.

With appetites aroused and pleasure-seeking as our only orientation, we are programmed to be taken by any little force that comes our way. The biggest joke of all is that we have the notion that we are the powerful ones--getting, having, and possessing all of the foods, tokens and pleasures that are dangled before us. Instead, we are being had, gotten, and actually possessed by the things that we think we own, seduce, or take. The irony is that these things which we have learned to find so attractive are actually the forces that are destroying the one aspect of power that we do have, and that is our freedom.

The voice of our freedom or "free will" is a subtle voice that makes itself heard only if we listen to it. There are only a few things that we do not have the power to resist or control if we can listen to this voice and use its power. The voice comes from inside, however, and it becomes necessary to adjust our hearing so that we can listen to the insides of ourselves. The superior powers of the human being are all inner powers. Our muscles, our physical appearance, even our sexuality are all very weak forces in comparison to the inner forces that move the muscles and interpret the physical reality.

These inner powers are the ones that must be developed both in the individual and on the collective level. With the development of these powers, we can achieve greater responsibility for both our individual and our collective lives.

In this section, we will look at some ways to re-open our inner ear, discover our freedom, and take renewed responsibility for our lives.

LOWERING THE VOLUME

Eliminating outer noises is something that we can do without "touching the knob," once we have gained our human strength. We will have the ability to eliminate the distracting noises simply by shifting our focus. However, during the time of our weakness (as most of us are now), we don't even have the strength to turn the volume knob down, that is, by actively changing our environments so that the outer noises don't disturb us. Therefore, we must develop some devices which will let us turn down the noise before we can learn to listen to the inner voice. How is this done?

For those who are interested in regaining their human strength, they have to be restrained from the noisy influences. It is sometimes necessary to institute strong prohibitions against certain types of music, movies, and distracting activities in our lives. Despite the child-like and, perhaps, puritanical quality of some of these restrictions, it is sometimes necessary to recognize that our humanity is in a child-like state and such treatment is necessary to elevate our awareness.

There is a real two-fold advantage that we have in this modern society. On the one hand, we have a choice to either grow or not grow. No one requires us to develop ourselves and there is considerable company (the majority of the population) that chooses not to grow. If you make the choice not to grow, then you are free to be a slave to the many influences that are anxiously waiting to take over your life. The second choice is whether you want to exercise control over your life or not. If you decide to take growth, then you will have to either place yourself in the proper ground for growth, or become a parasite and feed on someone else's growth.

Once you make the choice to grow, then you will have to exercise some control over the influences in your life. Therefore, you must determine that the volume of some of the popular music is simply too loud and the messages too destructive, and you must turn it off. You must decide that the images portrayed in the visual media are too distracting, and you must eliminate them from your experience. You can, of course, take the parasite's way and simply follow those around who have gained control over their lives and try to imitate whatever you see them do. This will not make you grow, but permit you to feed on other's growth.

Then there are those who wait to have someone force growth on them. They permit the influences to drive them to prison or drug treatment programs, mental hospitals, or some type of religious cult where a charismatic leader of questionable qualification dictates the controls over their lives. There are many people who cannot live outside prison walls. They live with considerable dignity and respectability as long as they have a guard over them but as soon as they must take responsibility for their lives, they find a way to get "re-canned." Such people make excellent puppets since they have already been conditioned to relinquish responsibility for their lives.

LISTENING TO THE INNER VOICE

Unfortunately, most people have come to fear the inner voices because they tell the truth about us. They speak of our fears and our weaknesses while also revealing our strengths. Most of us have learned to run before we get the strengths because we have become so afraid of vulnerability and weakness. Because we fear these inner voices, we quickly go back to the loud outer noises. For example, most of us cannot sit quietly alone in our room or ride in our automobiles without blasting the radio. Unless we are forced into solitary confinement, we have difficulty selecting solitude for reflection. Few of us take advantage of the quiet, early morning hours as an opportunity to simply listen to ourselves.

The beginning step to gaining contact with the inner powers that have been given to us is to conquer and restrict the outer noises that keep us away from ourselves. Because of the unfamiliarity of the inner voices, we may initially go to sleep, become bored, or simply turn the voices off. This is the role of discipline because to gain power over our worlds, we must first gain power over ourselves. It will probably be frightening for many of us to discover how childish we are and how difficult it is to regain control over our lives without giving them over to some type of outer influences. You will probably be amazed to find yourself rushing to turn your life over to something (a cigarette, a joint, a drink, etc.) or someone (a lover, a parent, a charismatic leader, etc.) to run it for you. The shocking discovery is that Erich Fromm, the famous psychoanalyst, was right and human beings do try to "escape from freedom."

Though we are fully equipped and capable of conducting our lives freely, we have become so accustomed to giving our lives over to other influences that we do not realize we have the necessary equipment. We actually run from the opportunity to exercise influence over our own lives because so many outer influences compete for authority. Despite honestly expressed doubts about the appropriateness of those authorities, people persist in giving themselves to them simply because of the habit and the carefully programmed appeal that they have for us. Experts in mind control, attitude manipulation, and motivational analysis who structure advertising campaigns specialize in inviting us to be controlled by the many outer influences available in this society. Of course, the potential profit which comes from having a large number of slaves is the most obvious motive for inviting people into such voluntary surrender of their freedom. Of course, there is the power motive, which is strong in some people who simply seek to control and exploit other people because it gives them pleasure. The idea of being popular and emulated serves as such a powerful appeal for some egos, that even without material profit, they delight in manipulating people's desires.

ACCEPTING FREEDOM

Once we have decided to accept our freedom and not try to escape it, we have the huge job of taking responsibility for our freedom. This is what is so frightening about reducing the outer influences over our lives. Most of us don't know what to do with our lives when we have the opportunity to conduct them. The Creator has given us authority over our lives and over much of the creation, but only a few are *human* enough to exercise that authority.

The important thing to believe and remember is that our proper orientation has been set. We need not fear where our lives will

17

go if we re-establish control over them. The problem is not with the direction that will emerge with freedom, but from the slavery with which we find such comfort. People who control their lives don't have problems. The people who have problems are the ones who let other influences control their lives. The alcoholic has problems because he lets alcohol control him. The hoodlum has problems because he lets his criminal and greedy influences control him. The prostitute has problems because she lets her pimp control her. Once we have come to listen to the inner voice of freedom and will, our choices will be consistent with the correct direction for our growth. Growth is a natural process. Stagnation is unnatural!

The voice of freedom and will grows louder with practice. Since our ears have been turned away from the inner voice, it is difficult to hear, at least, initially. The very act of directly turning off the disturbing outer influences makes it easier to hear the inner sounds. The practice of listening to ourselves makes our ability to hear ourselves improve. In other words, self-control improves self-control. The exercise of will increases the strength of will. The exercise of freedom makes us free.

The big task of taking responsibility for ourselves forces us to be creative. We must search within for the direction which offers us fulfillment and gratification. We must seek to entertain ourselves using our own intellect rather than relying on someone else's intellect. We must seek out people who foster our growth, rather than dragging us deeper into the fad of influences. When we look to others, we must not do it as apes who imitate, but in search of ways to direct ourselves. Our time must be utilized in free endeavors, rather than the slavish endeavors of doing what the influences have told us to do. Again, this is difficult at first, because we are so unaccustomed to being responsible for ourselves, the door to creativity is open for us.

AFRICAN-AMERICAN FREEDOM

Up until this point in this discussion, we have dealt with the problem and process of gaining control over our individual lives. The problem is a serious one and is responsible for many of the difficulties that we confront in our community lives. The disastrous number of teenage pregnancies, divorces, alcoholism, drug abuse, suicides, imprisonment of young Black men, and even economic problems can be understood as symptoms of African-American lives out of control. The group problem is no more than the individual problem multiplied as the individual problem is the group problem reduced. We need to work on resolving both the individual and the group problems at the same time.

African-Americans have been essentially controlled by outer influences since being brought to North America. (In fact, all Americans are, but the influences operate at some advantage for European-Americans). Since we, as a community, are so accustomed to listening to the outer noises, we can't listen to the inner voice of our own ethnic and community life. A pattern set in slavery persists as we listen to the directions and influences established by the former slavemasters. During slavery, the responsibility for our lives was taken from us so that we would accept the authority of the enslavers. The information and the voice of our own historical and cultural experience was silenced by the slavemasters. If we could have heard the voice of our own history (ancestors), our own religion, our own culture, then we could have remained free. Freedom was not given up willingly, but it was taken from us.

The problem that faces us in the second century after political emancipation is the need for psychological emancipation. We have not regained our freedom because we have not learned to listen to the inner voice of ourselves. We still listen only to the ideas, interpretations, explanations, and directions that are given to us from outside of our communities. Of course, that outer voice, like all of the outer influences, is much louder so it usually drowns out the small voice of freedom from within that has been stifled for almost 400 years. It is not an easy thing to hear the inner community voice, but freedom does not come until we hear it.

It is, therefore, necessary to turn off the outer influences in much the same way that, individually, we must turn off the radios and televisions that drive us away from freedom. We must identify the independent voice that comes from ourselves in order to locate the road to freedom. Every community has an independent voice. It is the independent voice of a people that is expressed in their culture. Once they hear the voice of their own culture, then (and only then), will they gain respect from other cultural groups. The independent voice does not require us to dominate anyone else, but it does require us to dominate (or control) ourselves.

The first step towards hearing the voice from within is to know that there is such a voice. That is the purpose of publications such as this one, and all of the efforts of many of the scholars and leaders who have encouraged us to recognize our independent identity. Carter G. Woodson, W. E. B. DuBois, Marcus Garvey, Elijah Muhammad, Malcolm Shabazz, Louis Farrakhan, and many others have strongly reminded us that we have an independent community voice that was silenced in slavery. They have correctly insisted that we can come into power, self-control, and genuine freedom only when we recognize and respond to that inner voice.

That inner voice is a history of experiences, a multitude of determined ancestors who cherished freedom, and a culture that has developed out of the efforts to obtain and maintain freedom. The inner voice is a compassion for each other, a commitment to the Creator, a respect for nature's laws, and a spirit that has refused to be defeated. The inner voice is self-love and an appreciation for a beauty and a being that goes back to the very origin of human time.

The inner voice of the African-American community can be heard when we speak to our children about who they are. We must develop independent settings for educating our children. Training is all right from the public schools, but education must be controlled by us. We must develop music, art, and drama, which praises our view of the world. We must encourage and support scholarship which explores our origins, triumphs, and defeats. We need institutions established for the study and preservation of African-American life and freedom.

We need to give support to the voices which speak from the perspective of our community development. Voices which invite us to give up our freedom to join in someone else's freedom is a voice of the outer world inviting us to destruction. We must listen to the voices which are consistent with the strengths of our past and yet offer an awareness of the present and the future. We must respect the voices of leadership which elevate us in dignity and strongly question those that would have us degrade ourselves in any form or fashion.

As we learn to listen to our individual inner voice, we can better hear the community's inner voice. The voice from within is the voice of freedom, and in listening to ourselves, we learn to take responsibility for ourselves.

THE POWER OF

SELF-KNOWLEDGE

Knowing ourselves is a fundamental aspect of assuming personal power and effectiveness. An essential job which cultures should perform is to teach people the knowledge of themselves. The way that parents raise their children, the things that are taught in school, the rituals, holidays, and ceremonies which occur in a culture, should all be directed towards developing the people's knowledge of who they are.

Human beings are not born with automatic knowledge of who they are, what they have been, and what they can become. This is taught by the society through the family, the educational structures, the culture, the symbols, and the religion of a people. Human beings develop on the basis of the information that they receive about themselves. If they are taught that they are people of dignity, power and value and are given examples of such characteristics in the people around them, then they become dignified, powerful, and valuable. If they are taught that they are inferior, degraded, and worthless, most of those so taught will become the outcasts of the society.

European-Americans receive a steady diet of their greatness as a people. Their homes and families display the symbols of European art, accomplishment, and dignity. The walls of their homes display pictures and structures of European and Caucasian excellence. Their cities are filled with statues, monuments, names, and structures which commemorate the heroes of their people. The media provides a constant parade of European-American beauty, accomplishment, and power. The schools teach Euro-American excellence in all spheres and all areas and times of human existence. Even their mistakes are shown to be accomplishments.

Is there any wonder that Euro-American Caucasians grow up expecting to have authority over society? Is there any wonder that Caucasian children are convinced of their superior intellect and appearance before they are twelve? Is it a surprise that European-Americans take control over their communities, over their lives, and over their institutions?

On the other hand, we teach African-Americans nothing about themselves. In the words of the late Elijah Muhammad, "The so-called Negro has been robbed of the knowledge of himself." We don't know who we are, nor do we know where we came from and we certainly have no idea where we are going. Without such knowledge, we are not only deprived of genuine power, but we are ill-equipped to develop power. We must continue to orbit under the influence of those who have power. Without power to change our lives and insure future alternatives for our children to meaningfully impact the society, we tend to see power as magical. We begin to attribute power to illusionary processes such as skin color, speech patterns, dress, material objects and similar superficialities. Without power, it is difficult to know that power is merely a by-product of knowing who you are and working in your self-interest.

People become what they are taught about themselves. Knowledge of oneself is the fundamental key to obtaining personal and group power. In order to deny people their human rights and power, the first step is to deny them knowledge of who they are and to fill this void with either wrong or negative information.

LOSS OF SELF-KNOWLEDGE IN SLAVERY

The American slave experience opened the books on this knowledge robbery of the African people. In destroying our cultural practices, taking away our names, language, religion, symbols, and rituals, we were stripped of knowledge of our human capability and accomplishment. After a few generations, our resistance to slavery was greatly diminished because we had no self-definition outside of being slaves. This was a necessary ingredient of the slave-making process.

We had no way of knowing that we were people of great accomplishment, power, and dignity. We had no way of knowing that our forefathers were the authors of civilization, science, and technology. We had no way of knowing that our condition in America represented a fall from power rather than a divinely decreed state. And, we had no way of knowing that we had the right to control our communities, our families, our economics, and our institutions just like the slavemasters.

Once we were robbed of self-knowledge, then slavery as an institution, was no longer necessary because we had become mental slaves. The only knowledge we had of ourselves was our degraded, dependent state and a set of myths which said that our origins were savage and God had decreed our servanthood to a "superior people." With no knowledge of ourselves, we accepted the European-American's knowledge of himself. We believed in his superiority in intellect, beauty, and power. Our only claim to accomplishment was to try to imitate him in appearance, thought, and action.

The knowledge of who we were was limited to our identity as slaves or humanly degraded persons. Our only hopes of personal value were to have a drop of Caucasian blood or to effectively imitate their manner. The knowledge of where we came from was reduced to a nightmare of uncivilized jungles. The knowledge of where we were going was either to the fields, up North, or to heaven. We had no knowledge of Black authority, dignity, power, or beauty. We did not aspire to be ourselves.

The impact of the slavery experience is discussed at length in another of my publications entitled, *Chains and Images of Psychological Slavery. (The reader is encouraged to review these ideas in order to see the far-reaching effect of this loss of self-knowledge on the African-American experience).* The African-American experience, however, could be replicated in any people who were removed from the knowledge base that taught them their nature, their history, their destiny, etc.

The African-American loss of self-knowledge did not end with slavery, however. It continues today as a process that had its modern genesis in the slavery situation. Those processes that are necessary for the restoration of viable self-knowledge have not been developed because of the post-slavery conspiracy.

THE POST-SLAVERY CONSPIRACY

As discussed above, self-knowledge comes to us through our families, through our culture, and through the educational and informational institutions of the society. Despite the tremendous attack on the African relationship during slavery, the ties of family were so deep, so broad, and so strong, that they were not completely broken. The power of mothers' love for their young was so strong that a message of human worth and dignity came through and transcended the oppressive conditions. The deep conviction of the spiritual structure of the world was so strong that faith and hope were not destroyed even when expressed through alien religious forms and symbols. The strength of love for children and the power of faith were the instruments which preserved some of our human dignity through ravishes of slavery and even up until recent times.

On the other hand, the culture and all that we knew from it, had another message. There were, and are, a few models of African-American power and excellence. When they occur, we have been programmed to ignore and/or destroy them. There are a few, if any, monuments, statues, or reminders of Black accomplishment. Even the walls of our own homes pay tribute to the accomplishments of European-Americans and often prominently display even a Caucasian symbol of God. (This is also discussed at length in *Chains and Images of Psychological Slavery*). Beauty is always the opposite of our most usual features. Power, in combination with "Black," is an obscene and militant declaration of war. This is the message of the culture from the parks of our major cities to the constant parade of European-American excellence on television.

Of course, the educational institutions completely omit the African contribution. Science, math, and philosophy are considered as completely alien from African-American capability. The great accomplishments in these fields are always associated with the images of Greece, Paris, England, etc. Even African triumphs in Egypt, Spain, and Portugal are claimed as an aspect of Caucasian accomplishment. Since we control almost none of the educational institutions (and simply imitate the European-American ones when we do), then we simply engage in the process described by Dr. Carter G. Woodson as "miseducation."

OUTCOMES OF SELF-KNOWLEDGE

Knowledge of self is more than just the recall of certain historical events and significant heroes. Self-knowledge, more than anything else, has to do with knowing how we, as human beings, work and what our real potential is. The historical and cultural events are simply examples of the best of human capability. Human goals and aspirations are defined by these cultural and historical images.

The outcomes of self-knowledge are many and affect all aspects of human life. These outcomes can be summarized in four general areas: 1) self-acceptance; 2) self-help; 3) self-discovery; and 4) self-preservation. The foundation for most of human productive activity is found in these four processes, which are direct outcomes of self-knowledge.

Self-acceptance is the beginning for all positive social activity. Knowing who you are acquaints you with the best of your human potential and leads to a productive acceptance of self. Accepting self means that you like self and you have a commitment to self. Accepting self means that you want to be yourself and not anyone else's self. The self-accepting person does whatever they can to express themselves. From physical features to cultural features, the objective is to express self. The non-self-accepting person tries to change their features to look like another self. For example, they might have their noses surgically "corrected" to look like the nose of another racial group. Rather than simply grooming and styling their hair, they may drastically alter their hair in a form to look like hair that they accept.

Self-accepting people recognize and follow those who represent their best self-interest. In fact, they willingly follow only those who have most clearly demonstrated a commitment to their highest interest. They respect the interests of others, if it does not mean working against their own self-interest. They are automatically disposed to support whoever demonstrates sincere concern in their interest.

Self-acceptance is the basis for unity behind constructive leadership. Love for oneself generates a commitment to one's cause and it builds a strong bond with those who share your interest in your group and goal. Genuine self-interest does not require you to hurt other's self interest unless that interest is in opposition to yourself.

There is an old saying that, "Self-preservation is the first law of nature." The evidence suggests that it certainly is a law of nature, but in the human situation, the first law is self-knowledge. Certainly, any life form that knows its nature either instinctively or rationally, operates in a self-preserving way. The key, however, is knowing one's nature, because without such knowledge, the law of self-preservation does not hold and people can and frequently do engage in self-destructive behavior.

The apparent contradiction that we often see among people who say that they love life, while actively abusing themselves in such a way that their destruction is certain, can be explained by this idea. It becomes impossible to engage in successful self-preservation activity if you don't know who you are or what you are. It's rather easy to accept your self-destructive habits if you are not aware that you have the ability to conquer any and all habits. Without knowledge of your group self, it becomes easy to engage in destructive behavior against the group without being aware that it is an aspect of yourself that you are attacking. Most self-destructive behavior, including suicide and fratricide, are illustrations of the self-preservation law gone awry. Such behaviors could probably be effectively countered through adequate self-knowledge.

Self-help is another rational fundamental human drive that again has its basis in self-knowledge. Human beings strive for independent self-mastery, not only in terms of their personal development, but also in their social development. The young child likes to tie its own shoe once it <u>knows</u> how. People like to take care of their own needs when they know who they are. Depending upon someone to supply their basic needs is a by-product of the type of slavery condition which requires that people must be deprived of self-knowledge. Looking to others to educate your children, provide economic resources, and to build your institutions only occurs for people without self-knowledge. People who know themselves want to fully care for self. Cooperation with others is certainly a part of self-help, but dependency is not. When you control none of the fundamental resources of your survival, then you are dependent. People with self-knowledge naturally revolt against such conditions, and are determined to do something for self.

The final significant outcome of human self-knowledge is the drive for self-discovery. Self-discovery is the process which maintains self-acceptance and actually continues to feed self-knowledge. It negates any opposition to oneself because it is an ever-expanding field.

Self-discovery is the fuel for exploration, scholarship, and all of the pursuits that guide our actions towards increasing the store of human information. Intrigued by the self-acceptance which has come from even limited self-knowledge, the person is actively motivated to know more about self in the personal and group sense. It is this desire for more knowledge that drives the development of expanding institutions, research, and the thousands of projects which characterize the search for knowledge.

People with a strong foundation in self-knowledge maintain considerable enthusiasm for acquiring ever greater knowledge. To discover more about self, in the broadest sense, is the motivation for most serious educational activity. Spurred by the drive for self-discovery, people give only minimal energy to any priority for knowledge which takes them away from self. Certain socially oppressed groups, when restricted in knowledge of themselves, expend excessive energy in pursuit of knowledge of their oppressors who they have often come to value above themselves.

The boundaries of personal capability are also challenged by this force of self-discovery. The person with limited self-knowledge and a consequently limited drive for self-discovery will be quite complacent in taking initiative. They will accept whatever limited definition they are given about what they can or cannot do. They will sit calmly among the mediocre, never challenging the so-called "handicaps" or restrictions on their activity. The person motivated by the drive for self-discovery will constantly challenge any limitation suggested in their capacity to act and alter their environment and themselves. They will never accept "can't" until an effort of self-exploration has proven its impossibility. Such people are always aware that there must be something else about their talents and capacities which have not been discovered. This driving force of self-discovery drives the person and a people to make real progress in the world.

"Knowledge of self" is more than a catchy phrase. The ancient masters of Egypt taught, "Man, know thyself." Ancient revelations and modern science agree that the real power in human capability is based in the consciousness of self or self-knowledge. As we have seen in this section, knowing who we are is the power of psychological, economic, political, and social effectiveness. People who know who they are can change themselves and change their world. Each person and each "tribe" must have self-knowledge if there is any hope of their survival and successful competition with the rest of humanity.

SELF AND SOCIETY

WORKING TOGETHER

In the process of adjusting to life, there are two fundamental mechanisms which must operate. One mechanism is the **person system**, and the other is the society system. This section will identify the basic characteristics of these two systems as they should optimally exist in facilitating the process of adjustment.

As was discussed in the first section of this book, the person is a very complex system having characteristics which are physical, emotional, mental, and spiritual. Ideally, for a living person, all of these dimensions are functioning and are critical to the life process. It is not unusual that at various points in the life cycle some of these dimensions demand more attention than others. It is also clear that in certain societal settings and historical periods, certain of these dimensions are emphasized more than others.

In this discussion, we will look at three characteristics of the person which must be taken into account in considering life adjustment. These characteristics are: 1) attitude; 2) self-concept; and 3) principles.

There are also three characteristics of the society which will be considered: 1) information; 2) respect; and 3) protection. The interaction between these characteristics of the person and the society are fundamental in affecting human development.

ATTITUDE

Attitude is a characteristic of the person which is fundamental to adjustment. Attitude is most generally understood as an inner state which affects our choices. Our inner responses to people, situations, and circumstances determine the kinds of choices we make regarding these things. A negative attitude results in avoidance and/or rejection, and a positive attitude results in attraction and/or acceptance. It has been said that "attitude affects our altitude."

Attitudes are affected by many things: information, experiences, other people, our own needs, fears, goals, and many other forces. Ultimately, however, attitudes are under control. We are capable of adjusting them positively and negatively through the power of will. The sense of powerlessness about out attitudes is often due to ignorance about the source and content of those attitudes. The more we know about attitudes and the origin of those attitudes, the better equipped we are to make appropriate revisions in them. The other problem is the lack of knowledge and respect that we have for our own ability to adjust our attitudes. We too often rely on other people or other circumstances when we might effectively seek additional information and proceed to alter our attitude by an honest re-appraisal and willful adjustment.

The attitudes we hold affect our choices, and our choices determine are relationship to life. We can control our attitude, and therefore, our choices. Attitude, then, is a critical characteristic of the person system that clearly affects our adjustment.

INFORMATION

The first societal characteristic that we shall discuss is information. The society (the culture, the system of the surroundings) has a critical quality of providing information. The information should be relevant to survival and relevant to the issue of adjusting to life. The society should inform the person of how people have resolved problems in the past, either through custom and traditions, or through formal education. It should inform people of what's going on now, and what circumstances surround them which require their adjustment. Finally, the society should inform people of their proper goals in order that they may be prepared for the events of the future.

The criteria for information from the society is that it must be accurate and honest. Information which intentionally conceals critical aspects of what has been, will misorient the person, giving them faulty solutions to pressing life problems. Deception about what exists makes people vulnerable to real dangers, and dishonesty about the goals creates false expectations which ultimately ill-prepare the person for what is to come.

The information must be relevant to oneself and to one's survival. An essential criterion for such information is the degree to which it reflects knowledge of oneself. If the traditions and customs are alien, if the education is irrelevant, and if the goals are dangerous to your life, then adjustment becomes almost impossible to achieve. (A later section in this book discusses education in greater detail). Attitudes are primarily shaped by information. Unless we accurately evaluate our information, we may have faulty attitudes based on misinformation. One of the ways to improve our attitudes and better facilitate our adjustment is to ensure that our information meets the above criteria.

Since information has such an important impact on the person system, it is frequently used as a means of misorienting the person. People who have rather thorough information of themselves operate rather effectively in accord with certain natural laws. People who are systematically or circumstantially deprived of self-knowledge are poorly equipped to adjust properly and appropriately.

One of the devices used for controlling people by controlling their attitudes is to control their information. Erroneous, but positive self-information, creates a people with an inflated sense of their capabilities. Either limited information, or erroneous information and negative information about the self gives the person a very depressed view of themselves and limits adjustment capability. The society system, through its control of information, can seriously affect the person system.

SELF-CONCEPT

Self-concept is another personal characteristic which is very important to life adjustment. Life adjustment is simply the process of attaining the greatest benefits from life. These benefits, of course, must be equitably dispersed physically, emotionally, mentally, and spiritually. Self-concept rests at the foundation of the person's capacity to reap the full benefit from their life. The greatest benefit is actually growth and natural development as a human being.

Self-concept is the way that we see ourselves. It is related to whether we see ourselves negatively or positively, usually based upon the information we have about ourselves and how others respond to us. Self-concept is the foundation for action as attitude is the foundation for choice. Two persons with the same resources, physically or mentally, produce differently depending on how they view those resources. The person with great singing talent who has an image of herself as a good singer will sing far more superior to the person with comparable talent but does not conceive of herself as a singer. The same is true with athletic, intellectual, or any special talent or human capability. We cannot necessarily be what we are not, but we become successfully what we are, based upon our concept of what we are. We fail at being what we are because of a poor self-concept.

Self-concept, like attitudes, comes from other people, our own experiences, and the kind of information that the society gives us about ourselves. If we get good and accurate information, so that we know our shortcomings as well as our assets, then we like ourselves and seek the best from ourselves. If we receive bad and inaccurate information, we dislike ourselves and expect little from ourselves.

There must be a balance in the construction of the self-concept. In part, we must rely upon others to reflect to us how they experience us. Therefore, we need honest and trustworthy sources in our societal environment to provide us with that information. On the other hand, the person system is equipped with its own reflective capability, and it must rely upon its own experience of itself. This requires a level of honesty which we must maintain with ourselves which grows out of a disciplined intention to cultivate ourselves properly. The ability to develop such an intention depends, to a great extent, on the kind to information that we have received about our potential as a human being.

Self-concept determines what we do with what we are. How we feel about ourselves is the major factor in determining how we are able to use ourselves. It is important, therefore, that we seek to obtain accurate information that gives us a good image of our best possibilities. It is with such an image that we make the best of what we are. Adjustment to life has much to do with what we feel about who we are and what we do with what we are.

RESPECT

Another critical characteristic of society is respect. The society should show respect, teach respectability, and be respectful of the person. A society is more than just an assemblage of people, it is a force. The force--as expressed through culture, tradition, and education--impacts directly on the person system. A responsibility of the society force and criterion for its legitimacy has to do with the quality of information which it transmits (as we have already discussed) and the respect that is communicated.

The social environment, if properly functioning, should stimulate all the persons within that environment in the same productive and satisfying way that the physical environment stimulates and feeds the physical system of the person. It must stimulate and activate the highest levels of expression. Therefore, a criterion for determining the adequacy of a society is the degree to which the genius, talent, and moral excellence produced in the society outweighs the dullness, mediocrity, and criminality produced in the society. When these latter undesirable human expressions begin to dominate, we understand that a flaw exists in society's communication of respect.

It is through respect that the self-concept is activated in a positive light. In the atmosphere of respect, the self-concept blossoms into the highest production of the most luscious human traits. Failure to generate respect for a person's self opens the door to human degradation. The respect experienced and expressed by the person is a reflection of the respect that it has received and learned from the society system. Respect is natural to the person system and in the natural support of a properly functioning social system, it grows in the person and facilitates the process of adjustment to life.

As noted above, the interaction between the collective self (society) and the individual self (person), is a highly reciprocal relationship. The more respect given by the social environment for the human being, the greater the respect that grows for the self. The greater the self-respect, the greater the respect for the society. We can see a direct relationship between the development of socially disrespectful attitudes and disrespect for the persons with these attitudes.

Respect, like information, must be accurately and truthfully based. Otherwise, people develop grandiose or overly inflated ideas about themselves and are incapable of practicing necessary human restraint. On the other hand, inappropriately based disrespect only creates a disrespectful response that eventually returns to attack the perpetrator of disrespect, i.e., hatred destroys the hater.

PRINCIPLES

Another characteristic of the person system is principles. Principles are those standards of conduct and evaluation which identify the aspirations of the person. Principles define the highest goals of the human possibility. Principles are the ideals which cannot be violated while seeking the best of the human potential. Principles represent the aspiration for strength and transcendence, despite a realization of the certainty of occasional weakness.

The person's principles are not intended to imprison him with guilt and prohibition, but to keep the way of ascending aspiration lighted. Principles are intended to light the way *up*, no matter how far down one might be. Principles are the guidelines, the blueprint for our humanity. A person without principles can only react, because principles are what attract us to action. Principles are bigger and more powerful than self-concept because they identify the best that we can be and not just an indication of what we are. Principles are the dreams that are never realized though they serve as the forces which direct our every waking act. They draw us ever onward, upward, and ultimately to the perfection of our humanity.

Principles are most often addressed through religious and legal codes. We are often made to believe that principles are external standards of conduct. They can be, but they shouldn't be, because principles should always be a living dimension of the person system. When principles belong to the person, the person is principled. The society helps us to develop principles though the ability to be principled is a characteristic of the person.

We should evaluate our principles carefully and be certain that they are ours. We should evaluate them against the figure of a perfect or an excellent model. We should compromise only those principles which are no longer worthy of our growth and our higher human possibilities. Principles should be the cooling breeze that soothes and disperses our aspirations.

We are well-adjusted when our attitudes and self-concepts are consistent with our principles. Our attitudes should be lighted by the principles which guide us. Our self-concepts should be evaluated by the best to which we can aspire reflected in our principles. Our adjustment and peace is a product of our work to bring these qualities of our person into order.

PROTECTION

To conclude this section, the final societal system character- istic that we want to describe is protection. Defense is a fundamental characteristic of all life processes and is crucial to resisting destruction of the life form. The society, as a collective entity, has a responsibility, not only to offer information and transmit respect, but also to protect the dignity of the persons within it.

The role of protection is manifested at its simplest level in providing protection for the physical welfare of its citizens. More importantly, the society system must offer, through its traditions, education, legal structures, and communication mechanisms, those kinds of stimulation which activate the highest aspects of the human potential. With such lofty stimulation, the person is protected from his own lesser tendencies. The society system must also discourage and exclude any hazard to the higher mental and moral possibilities of the person systems.

While protecting the higher qualities of the person, the society must also protect the freedom of the person to make choices. In the same way that one is not free to create a physical health hazard for other people, the society must prohibit persons from creating a mental or spiritual hazard for others. Though protection requires a collective responsibility to cultivate the highest life form for all persons, it must not violate freedom because such a violation hurts the active life process of choice, adjustment, and growth.

In the final analysis, the society system and the person system are one. The consistent interaction of the two processes is the continuing cycle of human adjustment which is as basic as the exchange of oxygen and carbon dioxide in the process of breathing. Attitude, self-concept, and principle are three basic processes which are shaped by, yet produce the collective society system. Information, respect, and protection cultivate the person systems, but are also created and controlled by persons. Adjustment is the balanced, honest, open, and consistent exchange between the two systems.

DIET FOR THE MIND

If one looks closely, one can find many parallels between providing for the physical body and providing for the mental body. Just as one must observe certain basic rules for the ingestion of foods into the body, one must also observe similar rules for the intake of thoughts into one's mind. The consequence of breaking certain nutritional laws is that we experience poor physical health and often considerable discomfort. Similarly, if we break certain laws of mental growth, we suffer from poor mental health. There are several basic characteristics of a physical diet which are also applicable to the mental diet.

In the same way that we must choose our foods wisely, we must carefully choose the experiences or ideas which enter our minds. One of the most serious causes of gastric disturbance is eating too much. If we fill our minds with too much of the material and experiences provided by this culture, we run the danger of mental discomfort in the form of depression or mental confusion.

This is particularly evident in relation to the use of television and other mass media. We find in these presentations a diet of mentally destructive material which, when taken excessively, will leave us very uncertain about what we should and should not do.

In fact, too much input of any kind is bad for our mental growth. This diet of excess provided by radio, television, and the rest of the media accounts for much of the complaints of boredom from many people in this society. We find ourselves conditioned for the constant stimulation by these media. The more we absorb, as the more we eat, the more we want. At certain points, it is important to refrain from feeding the mind. Silence and concentration are essential for a healthy mind.

One common complaint from many people is the difficulty which they experience in concentrating. The difficulty often is a consequence of clogging too much questionable material into the mind. Selected periods of silence produce the same purifying effect as do selected periods of abstinence from food.

Extremes in external stimulation weaken the reflective capacity of the mind. As we grow to rely increasingly on excessive amounts and intensities of external stimulation, we become less familiar with the quiet inner life. In the same way that excessive eating handicaps the body in properly assimilating material input, excessive sensory input into the mind handicaps the assimilative process of mental content.

In addition to avoiding excess, the mind's diet must follow proper laws of mental nutrition. With too much spice or too many sweets, there is gastric danger. This means, in terms of the mind, that too much fun and games is destructive to the growth of the inner person. We seriously retard our mental development by a constant diet of fantasy, partying, sport and play, which constitute the sweets of mental experience. Such sweets are necessary for proportioned growth of the person. If leisure and pleasure-seeking become the complete pre-occupation of the person, we run the risk of destroying our mental life. The mind's function is to solve problems and overcome obstacles.

A life of leisure has been made to appear attractive in a world which is overrun by material excesses. The value of leisure lies in its occasional occurrence between productive activities.

A constant diet of leisure activities begins to erode the seriousness and purpose in living. As a consequence, people begin to lose the desire to live and develop a constant boredom which leads to considerable unhappiness. Just as the attractive plate of assorted sweets is immediately good to the taste, in excess, those same sweets can cause much physical discomfort.

Inadequate amounts of the proper kinds of mental experiences can be seriously injurious to the development of the mind. Proper knowledge is knowledge of Truth and an understanding of the natural order of things.

A mental diet which fails to include adequate amounts of such knowledge leaves one's mind poorly formed and stunted in its development. Again, we find many examples of the consequences of poor mental nutrition in the present society which presents almost a famine in natural and spiritual knowledge. In the same way that a diet excessive in sweets leads to tooth decay and parasites, we find similar defects in man's social life. The tooth decay is seen in the disrespected laws and decaying moral fiber of the contemporary society. The parasites are seen in large numbers of criminal elements which fill the society at all levels.

Natural and spiritual knowledge is what is obtained by a study of the world in its natural form and study of the revelations of prophetic and wise persons. In a society which places such a high premium on artificial experiences from plastic flowers, to plastic love on television soap operas, we gradually lose contact with the natural environment.

There is much mental growth to be obtained simply from walking in a natural physical environment or growing real plants in one's home. Even something as simple as talking directly about our feelings to those with whom we come in contact, without the aid of music in the background or non-essential chatter, will stimulate our growth as a people. Such conversation will cause us to grow in respect for the feelings of other people and a recognition of the similarity in those feelings to our own.

The highest form of mental growth in the person results from the intake of Divine Wisdom. Such wisdom or Truth constitutes the universal structure of things. As we grow in understanding of that structure, we increase moral and mental strength. Moral and mental strength equips us for greater self-control and self-mastery. Control and mastery of self is the foundation for complete mental happiness and peace of mind. Mental peace within the people paves the way for peace within the society.

The abiding rule for proper diet is moderation. One might effectively parallel this rule to the mental diet. The ideal is the duly proportioned man. Such a man has been fed appropriately to develop as a balanced person. He is neither too emotional nor too serious. A diet which nourishes the mind on a fare of moderation raises that mind to a duly proportioned state.

VIOLENT TENDENCIES

FED BY VIOLENT WORDS

Mental images and experiences make us what we are. This information immediately begins to dismantle the fiction that evil and violence are a sign of the times, or a natural part of the makeup of people.

Many religions, the mass media, contemporary psychologists, and all of the major influences on our thinking have cooperated in convincing us that we are hopeless victims of our evil natures. After several episodes of the current fare on our TV screens, we are convinced, without debate, that humans, at our best, are basically evil. The majority of these super-violent presentations drive home the message that our nature makes us prone to violence and destructiveness. Many of the popular religious systems suggest that people are basically evil and that a violent death is the path of man's redemption.

The belief that evil, destructive and violent behavior is to be expected, makes us uncomfortably reconcile ourselves to an environment of blood and gore. We permit our children to absorb hours of violent rapes, killings, and sadistic mutilations from the movies and television. Then we wonder: "Why are the children so unmanageable? Why do they like to fight so much?" We erroneously conclude that there is something diabolical in their makeup.

The real answer is that we permitted them to be filled with words or images of violence, rebellion, and savagery. These "words" have shaped them and made them as violent as the Roadrunner, and as sadistic as Elmer Fudd is towards Bugs Bunny. We underestimate the power of the apparently insignificant experience of watching even cartoons.

History has well demonstrated that when a message of moral strength, basic goodness and kindness is fed into the minds of people, the so-called "natural evil tendencies" in man begin to disappear. When children are exposed to words of hope and high ideals, those children aspire for those high ideals of sharing, cooperation, and peace. The passive reaction to destructive and evil tendencies feeds the occurrence of those very tendencies. A resignation to such violence is the hidden message in the concept of the original sin, humanity's basically evil nature, and the unconscious aggressive drive hidden in people. All of these messages are erosive to the aspiring higher nature of human beings.

Fuel for such weakening messages comes from the constant input of weakness into the thinking of the people. One must first change the violent image of people and then change the "words" that shape us in order to reduce this violent disposition.

The lessons of history are making the world aware that the one predominantly natural trait in people is our infinite capacity for growth and improvement. It is only when we give ourselves over to our animal traits do we become like animals. If the mind is fed with spiritual wisdom and moral ideals, then it is possible to build a community of genuine moral strength and models of human excellence.

We have the obligation to remove ourselves and those for whom we have responsibility away from those influences that retard our growth. The more violence to which we are exposed, the more violent we become. The more evil we observe, the more evil we become. We should carefully select the kinds of experiences and people to which we expose ourselves.

UNNATURAL MENTALITY:

ROOT OF MENTAL PROBLEMS

Knowledge has been described as lights, and light is certainly that which permits us to see in darkness. No part of our world has been darker than the chambers of our minds. A characteristic of the Western thinking is its neglect of the inner chambers of the mind, while it focuses on the outer manifestations of the person.

Most thinkers agree that the source of people's basic psychological and mental problems exists in our ignorance of our own minds. Students of the human mind are almost unanimous in their recognition that the key to self-control, self-mastery, and mastery over mental confusion is a thorough knowledge of the inner workings and makeup of our minds.

The spiritual teachings brought by ancient religious teachers and prophets have served as lanterns in the dark caverns of our mind. Distortions of these spiritual teachings have often served to darken enlightened minds. As people begin to lose sight of the true meanings of spiritual instruction, they actually begin to bring themselves into mental darkness.

Many of us have not realized the many things which we simply take for granted as a direct consequence of the unnatural mentality which has grown from distorted religious teachings in Western society. Some contemporary religious critics have been quite explicit about the characteristics of this unnatural mentality which has resulted from a tendency to cling to the allegories of Divine wisdom as facts. The far-reaching influence of such childish thinking is not just destructive in our spiritual growth, but it has a very destructive influence on our mental health as well.

An example of how the unnatural religious mentality can cause mental disturbance is seen in the very common reaction to suffering. Each year many people spend hours and days of chronic unhappiness because of the confused religious notion about suffering. In the morbid story (or allegory) of how Prophet Jesus was supposed to have suffered is an unconscious suggestion. That unconscious suggestion is repeated in every image of the cross or crucifix! The suggestion is one which says to the unconscious mind: *IN ORDER TO BE GOOD, YOU MUST SUFFER.*

This motto of the suffering martyr Jesus has led to a fatalism about mental anguish and unhappiness which has overrun the minds of Western people. Many of us actually believe that to experience peace of mind and happiness in this world is equal to sin. Such people punish themselves by doing things that are of no value to themselves nor their communities.

The people have grown to equate suffering with the necessary price for sin. Coupled with the religious emphasis on people being born sinful, such suffering is accepted as an inevitable price for life. Consequently, it is not unusual to find people willingly subjecting themselves to all kinds of mental and even physical abuse because of the idea that suffering is necessary.

Many marriages are battlefields because the husband believes that the wife must suffer in order to show her love. The wife believes that love is shown by suffering, so she refuses to correct things in her life which would make her much happier. Relationships which should bring peace and happiness are assumed to be arenas for the working out of one's sins. For many people, a happy marriage is suspect. Some wives are considered neglected if they do not receive some form of abuse.

Mothers and fathers abuse their children because of the strong religious control on their thinking which teaches that only unhappiness and suffering builds character. The mothers and fathers, in turn, sacrifice their possibilities for peace of mind due to their need to suffer.

All such acts are done in the name of "God's" requirement that misery is righteousness. The continuing image of Jesus dying for the world keeps people convinced of the nobility of suffering. Therefore, they content themselves to suffer, rather than to seek peace as the real goal of life.

We can see that the subconscious messages given by the suffering image of Jesus on the cross has left a strong influence on the thinking of the people. The extent to which people wear suffering as a badge of honor has a destructive influence on peace of mind in the present world. People actively seek unhappiness and suffering because of this unconscious power affecting them.

As we seek more valid religious understanding, we become increasingly equipped to conquer not only spiritual problems, but social and personal problems as well. The unnatural religious mentality can be corrected by a more natural view of life and reality.

Those who use the words of correct scriptural interpretation as tools to excavate our own mental powers are discovering the power of light of understanding. The knowledge of the nature and range of the unnatural religious mentality on our thinking has equipped us to conquer and destroy such influences. Recognizing and beginning to understand this type of thinking is the kind of knowledge which frees us from things such as love for suffering.

A more natural view of life helps us to understand that suffering is not necessary for proper growth. Though difficulties and joys all feed into our growth, we are not required to suffer in order to grow into a firm moral sense. Human growth follows the same natural progression as all developments in nature. Nature actually provides a map through which we can better understand God's intended way for humanity.

Suffering, then, is not something that happens to us in such a way that we have control over it. Suffering is not something that we must endure in order to be worthwhile. In fact, it is our own controllable reaction to experiences which determines how those experiences will affect us. Our responses to our experiences are based on our view of those experiences. If a painful experience is viewed as a step in our inevitable suffering plight, we passively submit to that pain and experience it in all the intensity of its agony. If the same painful experience is viewed as an obstacle or lesson for self-mastery, we actively confront the pain and seek to overcome it. If we accept the pain as the natural signal of a need for some type of change of either a physical or metaphysical form, then we know that something must and can be done.

The unnatural religious mentality in the teaching that salvation requires suffering breeds a passive attitude toward pain. It simultaneously evaluates suffering as a Divine price paid for human salvation. Such teaching has given depression and unhappiness an unparalleled prominence in the contemporary world.

With the correct religious understanding, we have the power to create ourselves. This means that emotional reactions to experiences can be controlled by our conscious minds, especially when the conscious mind is armed with knowledge of the cause of such emotional reactions. Therefore, suffering is an experience to which we subject ourselves by our unconscious love for suffering.

This love for misery has been planted by unnatural religious imagery such as the suffering Jesus. We see ourselves as being Christ-like, not because our actions coincide with his teachings, but as our emotional response coincides with the image of his suffering.

DECAYING FAMILIES

One of the most serious problems confronting our communities is the increasing decay of our families. As serious as that problem is, it remains only a symptom of the much more serious problem of mental decay within ourselves. The problems confronting our communities are all indications of some basic problems of our thinking. By correcting them, we can eliminate the products of defective thought.

One of the products of such defective thought is the extensive and brutal cases of child abuse which have reached epidemic proportions in some communities. Another product of that seriously defective thinking is the increasing divorce rate which is also beginning to rise within affected communities. These are only two of the more alarming examples that those communities are in serious danger of self-destruction if something is not done immediately.

The family is the nuclear social unit in a Nation. All of the relationships in the society are based on the quality of life in the families and the lessons learned in those families. If families are closely knit, relationships throughout the society are closer. If respect for others is learned in relationships with family members, then respect is extended throughout the society.

A people's thinking is seriously affected by the ruling minds in their society. In contemporary Western society, this thinking, particularly in regard to man-woman relationships, has served to seriously erode family relationships. Families cannot be firmly put together until the men and women who serve as the basis for families come together in good and close relationships.

Because of the unreal images of manliness and womanliness portrayed by the mass media, men and women wrestle with the unattainable ideals of what they should be. African-Americans, bombarded with images of unreal macho men who are violent or have ambiguous racial and/or gender identities, are thrown into a kind of thinking which makes them desire to be something other than themselves. For the present rulers of society, this unreal image of manhood keeps the African-American male seeking to define his manhood in terms of some physical dimensions like fashions, gansta' skills, pimping, or a harem of women, or as the "mean, bad dude." Such an image of manhood keeps the African-American away from even desiring to be a part of the market place of world trade, production, or culture.

The woman is encouraged to aspire to become some thoroughly sexual, non-thinking receptacle for the whims of an equally unreal man. The woman and the man end up playing a game based on what they saw on television or in the movies. The woman is desperately trying to live up to some image of the tough, liberated, modern woman which is unreal.

Similarly destructive is the Hollywood and TV idea of love. When a people's thinking becomes controlled by such unreal images, they attempt to find "true love" in the romantic notion of some soap opera vision. When we discover that violins really don't play in the background when we kiss our chosen mate, we feel disappointed and unfulfilled and we soon begin to declare that we were cheated. We cannot recognize true intimacy which comes from within because we are constantly looking for the external signs which the movies have shown us should be there.

All of these problems stem from the false conception of men and women as material or physical beings only. The solution to our family and personal problems rests in our recognition of the inner life of our mental world where lies our true humanity and true love. If our man-woman relationships and all family relationships were conducted with an awareness of that higher moral purpose in man's development, then we could grow in true respect and love for both ourselves and for the physical distinctions between us.

EDUCATION OF THE

AFRICAN-AMERICAN CHILD

Educators almost unanimously agree to the need for a unique educational experience for African-American children. There has been a growing recognition over the last 20 years of inadequacy of the American public and parochial school system in addressing itself to the needs of not only African-American people, but increasingly to almost all of the American people. Education always has been recognized as the means by which a people gain control over their own thinking. This thinking should equip that people to satisfy and provide for their needs. The special cultural characteristics of a people require that they have a unique educational experience. At best, they can only use vestiges or adaptations of other people's educational concepts because each people's concepts have evolved out of their needs and characteristics.

Education, in its highest form, is no more than a process of attaining self-knowledge. One of the faulty assumptions that we have made in our attempt to obtain quality education for our children is to assume that we must assimilate the knowledge that has equipped other people to address their particular needs and utilizing the methods and contents of those people. We have assumed educational freedom to be the opportunity to imitate someone else's educational experience.

European-American educators know that true education is based on self-knowledge and the skills and methods of education should optimize that process. The Western man's power and knowledge is based on his mastery and manipulation of the physical or material world. There is real power in such knowledge, but there are also limitations. The fact is that the Western man has developed a system of education which capitalizes on his greatest strengths based on his self-knowledge. In that educational system, the Western man has placed himself in the center of the conceptual world. Historically, the world is recorded from the limits of his ascent into civilization, and scientifically the world is structured on the limits of his models of observation. This is not an objectionable trait of the Western system of education, but is instructive to educators from other cultural experiences. All valid systems of education have been geared toward furthering a people into the knowledge of themselves as a foundation for any other learning.

The African-American educator, in his demand for integrated education, assumed that in sharing the educational environment of the majority of citizens, that he would in fact obtain the same level of mastery of his environment as the European-Americans attained over theirs. This assumption has proven invalid and has served to even more effectively handicap the intellectual development of African-American children, than did the earlier system of segregated education. The response to such failures of the system has been a recent cry for community control of education. However, these community controlled settings have been similarly unsuccessful because of their continued utilization of both the content and methods of the majority system. Even with "community control" of the educational environment, if our content does not develop the self-knowledge of the African-American child, we have only a disguised system of providing some alien education.

It is essential that we not confuse the physical presence of African-Americans or non-African-Africans as the sole criterion for an integrated educational system. We must begin with a philosophy which cultivates African-American thinking for African-American survival (self-thinking for survival of self). Such a philosophy would have to define us in terms of our needs and on the basis of our identity.

THE IDEOLOGY OF EDUCATING THE AFRICAN-AMERICAN CHILD

We must address ourselves to several critical questions when we approach the education of our children. The first question is: *What shall be the ideology of educating the African-American child?* The answer to this question will guide our search both for content and methodology.

The Western educator has assumed the child to be essentially material. The educational process thus is viewed as the development of skills and information for the manipulation of the physical world. However, such manipulation has turned out to be shallow when we observe the polluting consequences, the unreliability of the products and the utterly destructive potential of such unguided technological effusion.

In a similar vein, we can see the inadequacy of just material skills in our own community. As a community of African people in North America, we are the most skilled African people in the entire world. We have a larger pool of resource skills than any other nation of African people on earth. Despite such an abundance of skills, we remain the economically, socially, politically, and psychologically most dependent people in the world. In terms of our ability to control our own environments and exercise control over our survival, we are the least effective people in the world. Because of this paradox, we can see more clearly the importance of education being more than skill development.

In order to properly educate our children, we must have an ideology which reflects the ideals and aspirations of our people. One component of such an ideology is the importance of seeing the child as a *Mind* developing in the environment of a physical body in a material world. Therefore, we immediately recognize the importance of devoting proper attention to the proper care of that physical body and environment. More importantly, though, we would move our attention away from the individual conception of the child which limits it in terms of its separate physical attributes. While continuing to be aware of the asset or limitation of those attributes, we would view the child more significantly in terms of its collective membership in the community of African-American people of which it is part. We would begin to judge the child's behavior, not so much in terms of its personal convenience (or our personal convenience), but instead, as a part of the enduring community or nation of which it is a part. Individual actions attain their significance by the degree to which those actions further or hinder the good of the community. For example, we would be more concerned about the selfishness of a temper tantrum than the personal annoyance of such behavior in an attempt to correct it. Rather than simply trying to change the behavior, we would want to teach the social consequences of such actions.

Our children must be equipped to avoid the propagandizing influences which direct them to self-destructive behaviors. Such influences as advertising and the mass media are concerned about furthering their own ends and are not concerned with the survival of our children. We are not so interested in counter-propagandizing our children as we are in developing such powerful images of themselves that they automatically counteract such destructive influences. As they develop love for the super collective self in the form of their own community, they systematically avoid influences which are destructive to themselves and their community.

In order to attain such reactions from the children, we must develop certain kinds of thinking processes within the child. We are concerned with the child's development of its inner self, its real self, its self as part of a majestic and enduring body (or tribe). The child's thinking is developed by the influences of its environment. Consequently, that environment should be constituted of a certain consistent moral climate. We need to develop in the children the kind of ethical mentality which makes them aware and respectful of a moral order in their universe. The moral climate should be one which operates on certain principles of respect and treatment of people as exemplified in the respect and treatment of the child. To cultivate that community consciousness in the child, it should be viewed as a community offspring, rather than just an offspring of its biological parents. The educational and home environment should be one that demonstrates a sense of collective responsibility both for the growth of the child, as well as its protection. The child, in turn, learns to see itself as secure in the community and responsible to all members of that community with the same respect that it gives to its biological parents and siblings. Such patterns of collective responsibility for child care and education were typical of our earlier history in the West, and are still practiced in traditional African and Asian societies. The loss of such a healthy pattern of child development is an example of dangers of imitating the patterns of an alien culture when one's mentality has not been shielded by a relatively thorough knowledge of self. It is only as a consequence of our present tendency to view the child only as a physical entity, rather than as a mental entity, that we moved out of that collective consciousness which permitted us to rear our children in this sharing modality.

The cooperative spirit that was the mainstay of traditional African societies and an instrument of survival in the slavery and oppressive environments of the West has been overwhelmed by the push for individualism. Individuality is a cardinal principle of the Western ideology and the increased assimilation of that value by African-Americans has sabotaged one of our greater strengths. An Afrocentric educational system must restore the principle of ujima (Swahili word for collective work and responsibility).

An environment characterized by kindness and discipline develops a sense of security and self-mastery. The Western society in its present degeneracy, has come to disparage self-control under an ethic of "do your own thing." Such an orientation has glorified the abandon of living in accord with one's passions rather than under the governorship of one's will power as cultivated in self-mastery. The majority of the world's people recognize the relatively greater power of mental and moral control over physical abandon.

THE CONTENT OF EDUCATION FOR THE AFRICAN-AMERICAN CHILD

The need for an ideology or a set of goals for the educational process becomes the basis for selecting what will occur in the educational setting. This brings us to our second critical question: *What shall be the content of education for the African-American child?* The content is guided by the ideology since the educational content should only serve to advance the child in terms of the ideals of the group.

Educational content should first of all be based on the realities of life or on what is real. The contemporary society has so glorified fantasy and synthetic things that they have become more attractive than reality. Programs such as *Sesame Street* exploit fantasy as a means of developing reading and counting skills. The assumption is that reality is not sufficient. Despite the superficial attractiveness of such methods, it places learning in an unreal context which though enjoyable, is deceptive. The present society's educational and social system has a tendency of indiscriminately combining fact and fiction. Such a combination has utility when fantasy is at least a symbolic representation of fact, but more often than not, the fiction takes our attention away from the fact and/or confuses the two. The unaware child becomes contemptuous of the real because it does not have the predictable smoothness of the false form. The child dislikes the real duck because it fails to talk like Donald Duck; it prefers the synthetic orange drink to the real orange juice because of its association with the fantasy world. Unfortunately, the involvement of the young mind with fiction rather than fact is ultimately for the purposes of exploiting them as consumers of things and ideas, rather than as producers of both.

If the child's education serves to alienate it from the natural world, it becomes disrespectful of nature and willingly abuses it. Environmental pollution, in the present world, is a painful illustration of such disrespect of the natural world. Another consequence is the pollution of self, both physically and mentally, when one becomes disrespectful of the natural processes of the body and natural powers of the mind. The rampant drug dependency among all segments of the society is a dramatic example of the problem of self-pollution which comes from a severe disrespect of the natural body and mind.

The person who eats and drinks body contaminants and seeks to counteract natural responses by additional chemical intake builds a vicious cycle which ultimately ends in premature death. The reliance on synthetic means for the alteration of emotional states shows a disrespect for the power of the mind to control its moods. Such abuse of the natural is a direct consequence of an educational system which trains the child away from the natural world.

Educational content should always focus on and draw from the form and processes of the natural world. Reading, science, and arithmetic should draw from natural occurrences as its root. The child should be encouraged to see that inventions and synthetic things are either discoveries from natural or adaptations of natural processes. This perspective is important for the African-American child who is too often awed by the mechanical ingenuity of the Western technologist and tends to be disappointed in itself because of the relatively limited control by African-American people of such technology. Children can learn through such an educational process that nature is the real benefactor and humans simply, by our mental powers, can utilize the gifts and lessons of nature.

Education for the African-American child should encourage observation and study of nature, so the child will learn of its equal access to the raw materials of the impressive empires of the present world. It is important that we sensitize our children to the origins of all things in the earth and in nature. In doing so, we provide the basis for our children to stand in awe of the real and in respect for creation, rather than fascination for that which has been drawn from nature.

Study of the natural world begins to encourage natural growth and development within the child. If they study the growth of plants, they begin to understand their own growth. If they study the cycles of seasons and the responses of nature to them, they learn of the cycle of birth, death, and rebirth without fear. By observing insects and lower animals, they learn the function of sex roles, work roles, and cooperation. All of these lessons from the natural world serve as the springboard for learning principles regarding the function of the world.

Rather than the child growing to worship the material world, they instead are equipped to look beyond the material forms in their origins. They can learn to respect the material world without becoming a slave to it.

THE SCOPE OF EDUCATION FOR
THE AFRICAN-AMERICAN CHILD

So we can see that our answer to the question of content reaffirms our ideology which is to develop the inner life of the child. The specific content becomes incidental so long as we follow the general guidelines of drawing from natural occurrences, natural processes, and building on these in our educational efforts.

We will gain additional insight into the question of educational content as we approach the third question of educating the African-American child, which is: *What shall be the scope of education for the African-American child?*

The scope of the African-American child's education should be the entire universe! It should extend to the limits of science and into the theology of time and space. Because of the minority status of the African-American child in the American environment, it is important that they see themselves from the perspective of a worldwide majority early in their education. Geography is a must, especially in conjunction with the appreciation of the value of land.

The child's perception of itself as a world citizen begins to counteract the limiting influence of the egocentric European-American perspective by its very prevalence. The child who sees itself as continuous with the inhabitants of the largest land masses on earth will necessarily have a much more positive perception of themselves.

Respect for the vastness of the universe and the inevitable order of all creation is also communicated through the study of astronomy. We want our children to be fascinated by the creation of space, rather than by the travel through it, because such perspectives begin to acquaint them with the vastness of their own mental potential. They are less likely to become addicted to the simple objects of man's construction. With such a broad scope of its worldview, the child begins to understand its purpose in life within a universal context.

Similarly, the study of history must reach beyond the recent boundaries of Euro-American civilization. Children must know early that George Washington may be the "Father of this Country," but the African is the father/mother of civilization! Children must understand that the roots of contemporary knowledge are found within the history of their own people. When the child is able to see the historical identity of itself and its nation of origin, it is much more adequately equipped to contend with the fictions of his present environment.

It is important for them to know of their history in America, but it must be presented to them, not as a totality of their heritage, but as a brief developmental phase in an extensive history. The educational scope should focus on the community of humanity, as well as the local community. Western education has a tendency to be very limited in its view of people and, inevitably, the norm for humans is the Western Caucasian man.

This perspective is one of the most destructive agents to the self-concepts of our children. It is crucial that the child views itself from the perspective of the world community of people, rather than the limited perspective of the present educational system.

With such a perspective, they are much better equipped to assess their behavior and that of others with more universal standards of right and wrong. This cosmopolitan scope to education is also accomplished by the learning of languages, particularly those which bridge the gap between African people on either side of the Atlantic. Particularly, a language such as Arabic, which semantically and phonetically is more reflective of the historical expression of the African-American than any European language. It would also tie the African-American to millions of African people throughout the continent, as French and German languages tie the European-Americans with their nations of origin.

Another vehicle for maintaining a broadened scope of the child's education is the study of world religions, their origins, and consistencies. In such a way, the child will view religion as a worldwide phenomena and not in the limited senses of somebody's invention. They will understand religion as a body of knowledge geared toward guiding the complete development of humanity. Biology, psychology, and religion should be taught as extensions of each other in the overall view of humanity as a developing knowledge form. That form is dictated by people's biological, psychological, and ultimately, their religious experiences. The interaction of these components constitutes the complete development of human beings. Such knowledge lays the foundation for proper human development.

THE METHOD OF THE AFRICAN-AMERICAN CHILD'S EDUCATION

The final question which must be considered in the education of the African-American child is: *What shall be the method of that education?* If the previous three issues of ideology, content and scope have been adequately addressed in the educator's study, then this final question will be one of the most limited significance. The method of education will, on the one hand, be dictated by the answers to the above questions and the method will be incidental to the questions of content, scope and ideology.

Generally, the educational method should be one that is as positive as possible. It should seek to build on strengths of the student, rather than constantly addressing its weaknesses. For example, creative attempts should be made to use the child's strengths in order to deal with its weaknesses. If a child has good reading abilities and poor mathematical abilities, the teacher can draw upon this reading skill to help motivate and improve its mathematical abilities, both by reading of the historical and natural occurrences of mathematical principles as well as studying ways of improving its own mathematical abilities.

Such a positive approach to education will build a love and respect in the child for education because they will view the school as a place for success rather than failure. The educational process should always be one that maximizes success and minimizes failure. The more positive rewards the child is able to receive for its involvement in the educational process, the more it will come to value its educational experience.

The educational setting should be structured but with reasonable flexibility for the varied needs and aptitudes of the various students. The teacher should be both comfortable and confident with their authority, but should always be willing to use nature or other insignia of truth as the basis for authority. The extensive educational experiences should make such resources of truth more available to them as teachers.

The child should always be encouraged to develop self-mastery. An educational process which involves excessive passivity on the part of the student, results in an over-reliance on outside sources for the acquisition of knowledge, rather than confidence in the child's ability to discover for itself. Again, this is why observation and involvement in nature becomes such an important tool, because it demonstrates the consistent availability of information for those who observe.

Children should always be approached reasonably. They should be viewed as developing minds with adequate reasoning and potential. Therefore, one should approach unacceptable behaviors, as well as acceptable behaviors with reasonable explanations as to why. In many instances, such explanations will not be convenient, but the child's integrity should always be respected. Structured and instructional discipline is necessary and should be utilized as a means of maximizing the growth of the child. It encourages his or her avoidance of emotional solutions to problems. This, of course, means that the instructor must utilize similar restraint in the administration of such discipline.

Finally, the most effective means of fostering the growth of knowledge within the child is by always attempting to demonstrate the relevance of that information to the child. Education should always be viewed and experienced as a means of widening self-knowledge and increasing the child's capacity to live effectively in his world. Therefore, it is critical that the material presented to the child always has relevance and applicability to the experiences of the child.

CONCLUSION

An effective educational system for the African-American child should have in ideology which sees the child as a developing mind housed in a physical body which should be cultivated for the greatest amount of growth. The content of that education should foster such growth by relying upon the natural and moral world as the best source of information regarding normal functioning and development. The scope of the education should be universal. This fosters the child's perception of itself as having a crucial and an ongoing relationship with all of the natural world and all of the universe. Finally, the method of education should be positive, structured, and relevant. This develops a respect and high evaluation for the acquisition of knowledge.

References

Akbar, Na'im. *Chains and Images of Psychological Slavery.* Jersey City: New Mind Productions, 1984.

Muhammad, Elijah. *Message to the Black Man.* Chicago: Muhammad's Temple of Islam, No. 2, 1965.

Woodson, Carter G. *The Miseducation of the Negro.* New York: AMS Press, Inc., (1933) 1977.

Biographical Sketch

Na'im Akbar, Ph.D.

Na'im Akbar is a Clinical Psychologist in the Department of Psychology at Florida State University in Tallahassee, Florida. He has been described by *Essence* magazine as "one of the world's preeminent African-American psychologists and a pioneer in the development of African-centered approach to modern psychology." A graduate of the University of Michigan, he has authored six books related to the psychology of African-American people and over 25 articles in scholarly journals. He is a past president of the *National Association of Black Psychologists.*

He has been lauded for his outstanding lectures at over 400 colleges, community settings and conferences throughout the United States, Europe, Africa and Asia. Akbar's luminary status has been facilitated through his numerous appearances in the national media including *The Phil Donahue Show, The Oprah Winfrey Show, The Geraldo Show, Tony Brown's Journal, BET's Our Voices,* and with significant articles about him appearing in The Washington Post, *The New York Times, Ebony Man, Essence, The Black Collegian,* and many other publications.

Other publications by Dr. Na'im Akbar:

The Community of Self

Visions for Black Men

Know Thy Self

Akbar Papers in African Psychology

Catalogues of Audio and Video recordings of Dr. Akbar's Lectures are available from:

Mind Productions & Associates, Inc.
P.O. Box 11221
Tallahassee, FL 32302

(850)222-1764
www.NaimAkbar.com

email: sales@mindpro.com